Daily Draw
Tarot Journal

This book is copyright protected. Please do not reproduce in either electronic means or in printed format except for your explicit personal use. This means that copying this book is prohibited and not allowed without permission from the author. All Rights Reserved.

Eclectic Blackbird Publishing © 2019

This Journal Belongs To

_____

Date:_____ Deck: _____

Question:_____

_____

Card: _____

⚪ Upright   ⚪ Reversed

Keywords: _____

_____

Standard Meaning: _____

_____

Initial Thoughts

Intuitive Interpretation

Emotional Response

How did this card play out today?

Evening Reflection

Date: _____ Deck: _____

Question: _____

_____

Card: _____
◯ Upright   ◯ Reversed

Keywords: _____
_____

Standard Meaning: _____
_____

Initial Thoughts

Intuitive Interpretation

Emotional Response

How did this card play out today?

Evening Reflection

Date: _____ Deck: _____

Question: _____

_____

Card: _____

○ Upright   ○ Reversed

Keywords: _____

_____

Standard Meaning: _____

_____

Initial Thoughts

Intuitive Interpretation

Emotional Response

How did this card play out today?

Evening Reflection

Date: _____ Deck: _____

Question: _____

_____

Card: _____

○ Upright   ○ Reversed

Keywords: _____

_____

Standard Meaning: _____

_____

Initial Thoughts

Intuitive Interpretation

Emotional Response

How did this card play out today?

Evening Reflection

Date: _____ Deck: _____

Question: _____

Card: _____
○ Upright   ○ Reversed

Keywords: _____
_____

Standard Meaning: _____
_____

Initial Thoughts

Intuitive Interpretation

Emotional Response

How did this card play out today?

Evening Reflection

Date: _____   Deck: _____

Question: _____
_____

Card: _____
  ○ Upright   ○ Reversed

Keywords: _____
_____

Standard Meaning: _____
_____

---- Initial Thoughts ----

---- Intuitive Interpretation ----

---- Emotional Response ----

---- How did this card play out today? ----

Evening Reflection

Date: _____ Deck: _____

Question: _____
_____

Card: _____
○ Upright   ○ Reversed

Keywords: _____
_____

Standard Meaning: _____
_____

Initial Thoughts

Intuitive Interpretation

Emotional Response

How did this card play out today?

Evening Reflection

Date: _____   Deck: _____

Question: _____

_____

Card: _____
   ○ Upright   ○ Reversed

Keywords: _____
_____

Standard Meaning: _____
_____

Initial Thoughts

Intuitive Interpretation

Emotional Response

How did this card play out today?

Evening Reflection

Date: _____   Deck: _____

Question: _____

Card: _____
  ○ Upright   ○ Reversed

Keywords: _____

Standard Meaning: _____

Initial Thoughts

Intuitive Interpretation

Emotional Response

How did this card play out today?

Evening Reflection

Date: _____   Deck: _____

Question: _____

_____

Card: _____
◯ Upright   ◯ Reversed

Keywords: _____

_____

Standard Meaning: _____

_____

Initial Thoughts

Intuitive Interpretation

Emotional Response

How did this card play out today?

Evening Reflection

Evening Reflection

Date: _____ Deck: _____

Question: _____

_____

Card: _____

○ Upright   ○ Reversed

Keywords: _____
_____

Standard Meaning: _____
_____

Initial Thoughts

Intuitive Interpretation

Emotional Response

How did this card play out today?

Evening Reflection

Date: _____ Deck: _____

Question: _____

_____

Card: _____

○ Upright   ○ Reversed

Keywords: _____

Standard Meaning: _____

_____

Initial Thoughts

Intuitive Interpretation

Emotional Response

How did this card play out today?

Date: _____   Deck: _____

Question: _____

_____

Card: _____
  ○ Upright   ○ Reversed

Keywords: _____

_____

Standard Meaning: _____

_____

Initial Thoughts

Intuitive Interpretation

Emotional Response

How did this card play out today?

Evening Reflection

Date: _____ Deck: _____

Question: _____

_____

Card: _____

○ Upright   ○ Reversed

Keywords: _____

_____

Standard Meaning: _____

_____

Initial Thoughts

Intuitive Interpretation

Emotional Response

How did this card play out today?

Evening Reflection

Date: _____ Deck: _____

Question: _____

_____

Card: _____
○ Upright   ○ Reversed

Keywords: _____
_____

Standard Meaning: _____
_____

Initial Thoughts

Intuitive Interpretation

Emotional Response

How did this card play out today?

Evening Reflection

Date: _____   Deck: _____

Question: _____

_____

Card: _____
   ○ Upright   ○ Reversed

Keywords: _____

Standard Meaning: _____

Initial Thoughts

Intuitive Interpretation

Emotional Response

How did this card play out today?

Evening Reflection

Date: _____   Deck: _____

Question: _____

_____

Card: _____
  ○ Upright   ○ Reversed

Keywords: _____
_____

Standard Meaning: _____
_____

Initial Thoughts

Intuitive Interpretation

Emotional Response

How did this card play out today?

Evening Reflection

Date: _____   Deck: _____

Question: _____

_____

Card: _____
   ○ Upright   ○ Reversed

Keywords: _____
_____

Standard Meaning: _____
_____

Initial Thoughts

Intuitive Interpretation

Emotional Response

How did this card play out today?

Evening Reflection

Date: _____   Deck: _____

Question: _____

_____

Card: _____
○ Upright   ○ Reversed

Keywords: _____
_____

Standard Meaning: _____
_____

Initial Thoughts

Intuitive Interpretation

Emotional Response

How did this card play out today?

Evening Reflection

Date: _____ Deck: _____

Question: _____

_____

Card: _____

○ Upright   ○ Reversed

Keywords: _____
_____

Standard Meaning: _____
_____

Initial Thoughts

Intuitive Interpretation

Emotional Response

How did this card play out today?

Evening Reflection

Date: _____ Deck: _____

Question: _____

_____

Card: _____
○ Upright   ○ Reversed

Keywords: _____
_____

Standard Meaning: _____
_____

Initial Thoughts

Intuitive Interpretation

Emotional Response

How did this card play out today?

Evening Reflection

Date: _____ Deck: _____

Question: _____

_____

Card: _____
○ Upright   ○ Reversed

Keywords: _____
_____

Standard Meaning: _____
_____

Initial Thoughts

Intuitive Interpretation

Emotional Response

How did this card play out today?

Evening Reflection

Date: _____ Deck: _____

Question: _____

_____

Card: _____

○ Upright   ○ Reversed

Keywords: _____

_____

Standard Meaning: _____

_____

Initial Thoughts

Intuitive Interpretation

Emotional Response

How did this card play out today?

Evening Reflection

Date: _____ Deck: _____

Question: _____

_____

Card: _____

○ Upright   ○ Reversed

Keywords: _____

_____

Standard Meaning: _____

_____

Initial Thoughts

Intuitive Interpretation

Emotional Response

How did this card play out today?

Evening Reflection

Date: _____   Deck: _____

Question: _____

_____

Card: _____
◯ Upright   ◯ Reversed

Keywords: _____
_____

Standard Meaning: _____
_____

Initial Thoughts

Intuitive Interpretation

Emotional Response

How did this card play out today?

Evening Reflection

Date: _____   Deck: _____

Question: _____
_____

Card: _____
○ Upright   ○ Reversed

Keywords: _____
_____

Standard Meaning: _____
_____

--- Initial Thoughts ---

--- Intuitive Interpretation ---

--- Emotional Response ---

--- How did this card play out today? ---

Evening Reflection

Date: _____ Deck: _____

Question: _____

_____

Card: _____

○ Upright   ○ Reversed

Keywords: _____

_____

Standard Meaning: _____

_____

Initial Thoughts

Intuitive Interpretation

Emotional Response

How did this card play out today?

Evening Reflection

Date: _____   Deck: _____

Question: _____

_____

Card: _____
○ Upright   ○ Reversed

Keywords: _____

_____

Standard Meaning: _____

_____

Initial Thoughts

Intuitive Interpretation

Emotional Response

How did this card play out today?

Evening Reflection

Date: _____   Deck: _____

Question: _____
_____

Card: _____
  ◯ Upright   ◯ Reversed

Keywords: _____
_____

Standard Meaning: _____
_____

Initial Thoughts

Intuitive Interpretation

Emotional Response

How did this card play out today?

Evening Reflection

Date: _____   Deck: _____

Question: _____

_____

Card: _____

○ Upright   ○ Reversed

Keywords: _____

_____

Standard Meaning: _____

_____

Initial Thoughts

Intuitive Interpretation

Emotional Response

How did this card play out today?

Evening Reflection

Date: _____ Deck: _____

Question: _____

_____

Card: _____
    ◯ Upright   ◯ Reversed

Keywords: _____
_____

Standard Meaning: _____
_____

Initial Thoughts

Intuitive Interpretation

Emotional Response

How did this card play out today?

Evening Reflection

Date: _____ Deck: _____

Question: _____

_____

Card: _____
  ◯ Upright   ◯ Reversed

Keywords: _____
_____

Standard Meaning: _____
_____

Initial Thoughts

Intuitive Interpretation

Emotional Response

How did this card play out today?

Evening Reflection

Date: _____ Deck: _____

Question: _____

_____

Card: _____

○ Upright   ○ Reversed

Keywords: _____

_____

Standard Meaning: _____

_____

---- Initial Thoughts ----

---- Intuitive Interpretation ----

---- Emotional Response ----

---- How did this card play out today? ----

Evening Reflection

Date: _____   Deck: _____

Question: _____

_____

Card: _____
  ○ Upright   ○ Reversed

Keywords: _____
_____

Standard Meaning: _____
_____

Initial Thoughts

Intuitive Interpretation

Emotional Response

How did this card play out today?

Evening Reflection

Date: _____ Deck: _____

Question: _____
_____

Card: _____

○ Upright   ○ Reversed

Keywords: _____
_____

Standard Meaning: _____
_____

Initial Thoughts

Intuitive Interpretation

Emotional Response

How did this card play out today?

Evening Reflection

Date: _____   Deck: _____

Question: _____

_____

Card: _____
　　　○ Upright　　　　○ Reversed

Keywords: _____
_____

Standard Meaning: _____
_____

Initial Thoughts

Intuitive Interpretation

Emotional Response

How did this card play out today?

Evening Reflection

Date: _____   Deck: _____

Question: _____

_____

Card: _____
   ○ Upright   ○ Reversed

Keywords: _____
_____

Standard Meaning: _____
_____

---- **Initial Thoughts** ----

---- Intuitive Interpretation ----

---- **Emotional Response** ----

---- How did this card play out today? ----

Evening Reflection

Date: _____   Deck: _____

Question: _____

_____

Card: _____
○ Upright   ○ Reversed

Keywords: _____
_____

Standard Meaning: _____
_____

--- Initial Thoughts ---

--- Intuitive Interpretation ---

--- Emotional Response ---

--- How did this card play out today? ---

Evening Reflection

Date: _____ Deck: _____

Question: _____

_____

Card: _____

○ Upright   ○ Reversed

Keywords: _____

_____

Standard Meaning: _____

_____

Initial Thoughts

Intuitive Interpretation

Emotional Response

How did this card play out today?

Evening Reflection

Date: _____   Deck: _____

Question: _____

_____

Card: _____

○ Upright   ○ Reversed

Keywords: _____

_____

Standard Meaning: _____

_____

Initial Thoughts

Intuitive Interpretation

Emotional Response

How did this card play out today?

Evening Reflection

Date:_____   Deck: _____

Question:_____

_____

Card: _____
　　　　　○ Upright　　　　　○ Reversed

Keywords: _____
_____

Standard Meaning: _____
_____

Initial Thoughts

Intuitive Interpretation

Emotional Response

How did this card play out today?

Evening Reflection

Date: _____ Deck: _____

Question: _____

_____

Card: _____

○ Upright   ○ Reversed

Keywords: _____

_____

Standard Meaning: _____

_____

Initial Thoughts

Intuitive Interpretation

Emotional Response

How did this card play out today?

Evening Reflection

Date: _____ Deck: _____

Question: _____

Card: _____
◯ Upright   ◯ Reversed

Keywords: _____

Standard Meaning: _____

Initial Thoughts

Intuitive Interpretation

Emotional Response

How did this card play out today?

Evening Reflection

Date: _____   Deck: _____

Question: _____

_____

Card: _____

◯ Upright   ◯ Reversed

Keywords: _____

_____

Standard Meaning: _____

_____

Initial Thoughts

Intuitive Interpretation

Emotional Response

How did this card play out today?

Evening Reflection

Date: _____ Deck: _____

Question: _____
_____

Card: _____
  ○ Upright   ○ Reversed

Keywords: _____
_____

Standard Meaning: _____
_____

Initial Thoughts

Intuitive Interpretation

Emotional Response

How did this card play out today?

Evening Reflection

Date: _____   Deck: _____

Question: _____

_____

Card: _____

○ Upright   ○ Reversed

Keywords: _____

_____

Standard Meaning: _____

_____

--- Initial Thoughts ---

--- Intuitive Interpretation ---

--- Emotional Response ---

--- How did this card play out today? ---

Evening Reflection

Date: _____ Deck: _____

Question: _____

_____

Card: _____
◯ Upright   ◯ Reversed

Keywords: _____
_____

Standard Meaning: _____
_____

Initial Thoughts

Intuitive Interpretation

Emotional Response

How did this card play out today?

Evening Reflection

Date: _____ Deck: _____

Question: _____

_____

Card: _____

○ Upright   ○ Reversed

Keywords: _____

_____

Standard Meaning: _____

_____

Initial Thoughts

Intuitive Interpretation

Emotional Response

How did this card play out today?

Evening Reflection

Date: _____   Deck: _____

Question: _____

_____

Card: _____
◯ Upright   ◯ Reversed

Keywords: _____
_____

Standard Meaning: _____
_____

Initial Thoughts

Intuitive Interpretation

Emotional Response

How did this card play out today?

Evening Reflection

Date: _____ Deck: _____

Question: _____

_____

Card: _____
    ○ Upright   ○ Reversed

Keywords: _____
_____

Standard Meaning: _____
_____

---- **Initial Thoughts** ----

---- **Intuitive Interpretation** ----

---- **Emotional Response** ----

---- **How did this card play out today?** ----

Evening Reflection

Date: _____ Deck: _____

Question: _____

_____

Card: _____

○ Upright ○ Reversed

Keywords: _____

_____

Standard Meaning: _____

_____

Initial Thoughts

Intuitive Interpretation

Emotional Response

How did this card play out today?

Evening Reflection

Date: _____ Deck: _____

Question: _____

_____

Card: _____
○ Upright   ○ Reversed

Keywords: _____
_____

Standard Meaning: _____
_____

Initial Thoughts

Intuitive Interpretation

Emotional Response

How did this card play out today?

Evening Reflection

Date: _____   Deck: _____

Question: _____

_____

Card: _____
   ○ Upright   ○ Reversed

Keywords: _____
_____

Standard Meaning: _____
_____

Initial Thoughts

Intuitive Interpretation

Emotional Response

How did this card play out today?

Evening Reflection

Date: _____ Deck: _____

Question: _____
_____

Card: _____
○ Upright   ○ Reversed

Keywords: _____
_____

Standard Meaning: _____
_____

--[Initial Thoughts]--

--[Intuitive Interpretation]--

--[Emotional Response]--

--[How did this card play out today?]--

Evening Reflection

Date: _____   Deck: _____

Question: _____

_____

Card: _____
  ○ Upright   ○ Reversed

Keywords: _____
_____

Standard Meaning: _____
_____

Initial Thoughts

Intuitive Interpretation

Emotional Response

How did this card play out today?

Evening Reflection

Date: _____ Deck: _____

Question: _____

_____

Card: _____

◯ Upright   ◯ Reversed

Keywords: _____
_____

Standard Meaning: _____
_____

Initial Thoughts

Intuitive Interpretation

Emotional Response

How did this card play out today?

Evening Reflection

Date: _____ Deck: _____

Question: _____

_____

Card: _____
○ Upright   ○ Reversed

Keywords: _____
_____

Standard Meaning: _____
_____

Initial Thoughts

Intuitive Interpretation

Emotional Response

How did this card play out today?

Evening Reflection

Date: _____ Deck: _____

Question: _____

_____

Card: _____

◯ Upright   ◯ Reversed

Keywords: _____

_____

Standard Meaning: _____

_____

---- **Initial Thoughts** ----

---- **Intuitive Interpretation** ----

---- **Emotional Response** ----

---- **How did this card play out today?** ----

Evening Reflection

Date: _____ Deck: _____

Question: _____

_____

Card: _____
○ Upright   ○ Reversed

Keywords: _____
_____

Standard Meaning: _____
_____

Initial Thoughts

Intuitive Interpretation

Emotional Response

How did this card play out today?

Evening Reflection

Date:_____   Deck:_____

Question:_____
_____

Card: _____
  ○ Upright   ○ Reversed

Keywords: _____
_____

Standard Meaning: _____
_____

Initial Thoughts

Intuitive Interpretation

Emotional Response

How did this card play out today?

Evening Reflection

Date:_____ Deck: _____

Question:_____

_____

Card: _____
    ○ Upright   ○ Reversed

Keywords: _____

_____

Standard Meaning: _____

_____

Initial Thoughts

Intuitive Interpretation

Emotional Response

How did this card play out today?

Evening Reflection

Date: _____ Deck: _____

Question: _____

_____

Card: _____
- ○ Upright   ○ Reversed

Keywords: _____
_____

Standard Meaning: _____
_____

--- Initial Thoughts ---

--- Intuitive Interpretation ---

--- Emotional Response ---

--- How did this card play out today? ---

Evening Reflection

Date: _____ Deck: _____

Question: _____

_____

Card: _____

◯ Upright   ◯ Reversed

Keywords: _____

_____

Standard Meaning: _____

_____

Initial Thoughts

Intuitive Interpretation

Emotional Response

How did this card play out today?

Evening Reflection

Date: _____ Deck: _____

Question: _____

_____

Card: _____
○ Upright   ○ Reversed

Keywords: _____
_____

Standard Meaning: _____
_____

Initial Thoughts

Intuitive Interpretation

Emotional Response

How did this card play out today?

Evening Reflection

Date: _____   Deck: _____

Question: _____

_____

Card: _____
   ○ Upright   ○ Reversed

Keywords: _____
_____

Standard Meaning: _____
_____

Initial Thoughts

Intuitive Interpretation

Emotional Response

How did this card play out today?

Evening Reflection

Date: _____ Deck: _____

Question: _____

_____

Card: _____

○ Upright   ○ Reversed

Keywords: _____
_____

Standard Meaning: _____
_____

Initial Thoughts

Intuitive Interpretation

Emotional Response

How did this card play out today?

Evening Reflection

Date: _____   Deck: _____

Question: _____

_____

Card: _____
　　　○ Upright　　　　○ Reversed

Keywords: _____
_____

Standard Meaning: _____
_____

Initial Thoughts

Intuitive Interpretation

Emotional Response

How did this card play out today?

Evening Reflection

Date: _____ Deck: _____

Question: _____

_____

Card: _____
○ Upright   ○ Reversed

Keywords: _____
_____

Standard Meaning: _____
_____

--- Initial Thoughts ---

--- Intuitive Interpretation ---

--- Emotional Response ---

--- How did this card play out today? ---

Evening Reflection

Date: _____   Deck: _____

Question: _____
_____

Card: _____
　　　○ Upright　　　　　○ Reversed

Keywords: _____
_____

Standard Meaning: _____
_____

Initial Thoughts

Intuitive Interpretation

Emotional Response

How did this card play out today?

Evening Reflection

Date: _____ Deck: _____

Question: _____

_____

Card: _____
○ Upright   ○ Reversed

Keywords: _____
_____

Standard Meaning: _____
_____

Initial Thoughts

Intuitive Interpretation

Emotional Response

How did this card play out today?

Evening Reflection

Date: _____ Deck: _____

Question: _____

_____

Card: _____

○ Upright   ○ Reversed

Keywords: _____

_____

Standard Meaning: _____

_____

Initial Thoughts

Intuitive Interpretation

Emotional Response

How did this card play out today?

Evening Reflection

Date: _____   Deck: _____

Question: _____

_____

Card: _____

○ Upright   ○ Reversed

Keywords: _____

_____

Standard Meaning: _____

_____

Initial Thoughts

Intuitive Interpretation

Emotional Response

How did this card play out today?

Evening Reflection

Date: _____ Deck: _____

Question: _____
_____

Card: _____
　　　○ Upright　　　　○ Reversed

Keywords: _____
_____

Standard Meaning: _____
_____

--- Initial Thoughts ---

--- Intuitive Interpretation ---

--- Emotional Response ---

--- How did this card play out today? ---

Evening Reflection

Date: _____   Deck: _____

Question: _____

_____

Card: _____

○ Upright   ○ Reversed

Keywords: _____
_____

Standard Meaning: _____
_____

---- Initial Thoughts ----

---- Intuitive Interpretation ----

---- Emotional Response ----

---- How did this card play out today? ----

Evening Reflection

Date: _____   Deck: _____

Question: _____
_____

Card: _____
  ◯ Upright   ◯ Reversed

Keywords: _____
_____

Standard Meaning: _____
_____

Initial Thoughts

Intuitive Interpretation

Emotional Response

How did this card play out today?

Evening Reflection

Date:_____   Deck:_____

Question:_____

_____

Card: _____
○ Upright   ○ Reversed

Keywords: _____
_____

Standard Meaning: _____
_____

Initial Thoughts

Intuitive Interpretation

Emotional Response

How did this card play out today?

Evening Reflection

Date: _____ Deck: _____

Question: _____

_____

Card: _____
    ◯ Upright   ◯ Reversed

Keywords: _____
_____

Standard Meaning: _____
_____

Initial Thoughts

Intuitive Interpretation

Emotional Response

How did this card play out today?

Evening Reflection

Date: _____   Deck: _____

Question: _____
_____

Card: _____
○ Upright   ○ Reversed

Keywords: _____
_____

Standard Meaning: _____
_____

Initial Thoughts

Intuitive Interpretation

Emotional Response

How did this card play out today?

Evening Reflection

Date: _____   Deck: _____

Question: _____

_____

Card: _____
    ◯ Upright   ◯ Reversed

Keywords: _____

_____

Standard Meaning: _____

_____

Initial Thoughts

Intuitive Interpretation

Emotional Response

How did this card play out today?

Evening Reflection

Date: _____ Deck: _____

Question: _____

_____

Card: _____
◯ Upright   ◯ Reversed

Keywords: _____
_____

Standard Meaning: _____
_____

--- Initial Thoughts ---

--- Intuitive Interpretation ---

--- Emotional Response ---

--- How did this card play out today? ---

Evening Reflection

Date: _____ Deck: _____

Question: _____

_____

Card: _____
○ Upright   ○ Reversed

Keywords: _____
_____

Standard Meaning: _____
_____

Initial Thoughts

Intuitive Interpretation

Emotional Response

How did this card play out today?

Evening Reflection

Date: _____   Deck: _____

Question: _____

_____

Card: _____
　　　○ Upright　　　　○ Reversed

Keywords: _____
_____

Standard Meaning: _____
_____

Initial Thoughts

Intuitive Interpretation

Emotional Response

How did this card play out today?

Evening Reflection

Date: _____ Deck: _____

Question: _____

_____

Card: _____
○ Upright   ○ Reversed

Keywords: _____

_____

Standard Meaning: _____

_____

--- Initial Thoughts ---

--- Intuitive Interpretation ---

--- Emotional Response ---

--- How did this card play out today? ---

Evening Reflection

Date: _____ Deck: _____

Question: _____

_____

Card: _____
　　　○ Upright　　　　○ Reversed

Keywords: _____
_____

Standard Meaning: _____
_____

Initial Thoughts

Intuitive Interpretation

Emotional Response

How did this card play out today?

Evening Reflection

Date: _____   Deck: _____

Question: _____
_____

Card: _____

◯ Upright   ◯ Reversed

Keywords: _____
_____

Standard Meaning: _____
_____

Initial Thoughts

Intuitive Interpretation

Emotional Response

How did this card play out today?

Evening Reflection

Date: _____ Deck: _____

Question: _____

_____

Card: _____
○ Upright   ○ Reversed

Keywords: _____
_____

Standard Meaning: _____
_____

Initial Thoughts

Intuitive Interpretation

Emotional Response

How did this card play out today?

Evening Reflection

Date: _____   Deck: _____

Question: _____

_____

Card: _____

◯ Upright   ◯ Reversed

Keywords: _____

_____

Standard Meaning: _____

_____

--- Initial Thoughts ---

--- Intuitive Interpretation ---

--- Emotional Response ---

--- How did this card play out today? ---

Evening Reflection

Date: _____   Deck: _____

Question: _____

_____

Card: _____
   ○ Upright   ○ Reversed

Keywords: _____
_____

Standard Meaning: _____
_____

--- Initial Thoughts ---

--- Intuitive Interpretation ---

--- Emotional Response ---

--- How did this card play out today? ---

Evening Reflection

Date: _____   Deck: _____

Question: _____

_____

Card: _____
    ○ Upright   ○ Reversed

Keywords: _____
_____

Standard Meaning: _____
_____

Initial Thoughts

Intuitive Interpretation

Emotional Response

How did this card play out today?

Evening Reflection